United States Government Accountability Office

Report to Congressional Requesters

I0448587

June 2013

GRANT WORKFORCE

Agency Training Practices Should Inform Future Government-wide Efforts

June 2013

GAO Highlights

Highlights of GAO-13-591, a report to congressional requesters

GRANT WORKFORCE

Agency Training Practices Should Inform Future Government-wide Efforts

Why GAO Did This Study

Grants are a key tool used by the federal government to achieve a wide variety of national objectives. However, there are no government-wide training standards or requirements for the federal grant workforce. COFAR has reported it plans to develop such standards. GAO was asked to describe how the grant workforce is trained and what challenges and good practices exist. This report (1) describes the federal grant workforce at selected agencies and analyzes the challenge of identifying the workforce government-wide and (2) examines selected good practices agencies use and challenges, if any, in grants training and the potential implications for developing government-wide grants training standards. GAO obtained government-wide information on grants training through a questionnaire to chief learning officers at 22 federal agencies. For in-depth illustrative examples of grants training practices and challenges, GAO selected four agencies—Education, HHS, State, and DOT—based on factors such as total grant obligations and the number and type of grant programs administered. GAO also reviewed documentation and interviewed officials at OMB and OPM.

What GAO Recommends

GAO is making recommendations to the Director of OMB regarding the importance of including both types of grants management roles—grants management specialists and program specialists—when developing government-wide grants management competencies and certification standards.

OMB staff concurred with the recommendations.

View GAO-13-591. For more information, contact Stanley J. Czerwinski at (202) 512-6806 or czerwinskis@gao.gov

What GAO Found

Identifying the federal grant workforce presents challenges due to differences in how agencies manage grants and the wide range of job series that make up the grant workforce. Some agencies manage grants by using a combination of program specialists (subject-matter experts) and grants management specialists, while other agencies use program specialists to manage the entire grant process. In the four agencies that GAO focused on for this review—the Departments of Education (Education), Health and Human Services (HHS), State (State), and Transportation (DOT)—agency officials identified over 5,100 employees who were significantly involved in managing grants, spanning more than 50 different occupational job series. Recognizing the need for a classification that would more accurately capture the work of federal employees who manage grants, in 2010 the Office of Personnel Management (OPM) created the "Grants Management Specialist" job series. However, due to the different ways that agencies manage grants, the extent to which agencies have adopted this series varies widely. More than half of the 22 federal grant-making agencies GAO surveyed make limited or no use of the job series. The Council on Financial Assistance Reform (COFAR), established by the Office of Management and Budget (OMB) in October 2011 to provide recommendations on grants policy and management reforms, has announced plans to develop government-wide grants training standards, but it has not released information on how it plans to define the grant workforce. Defining the grant workforce is an important step in developing an effective government-wide grants training strategy.

Agency officials identified three key practices to develop the grant workforce: (1) competencies, (2) agency-specific training, and (3) certification programs. First, some agencies developed their own competency models in order to better reflect the way they assigned grants management responsibilities. Officials at these agencies told GAO that OPM's grants management competency model was not directly applicable to employees carrying out the program specialist role in their organizations. For example, rather than apply OPM's competency model, a component of HHS developed a separate competency model tailored to program specialist employees responsible for managing grants. Second, agencies addressed their grants training needs through courses and other training mechanisms designed to provide knowledge of agency-specific policies and procedures. Officials reported challenges finding grants training that met all the needs of the grant workforce, and responded to this by customizing grants training courses. For example, Education customized commercial courses to include agency-specific policies and procedures and a component of HHS developed its own grants management courses to achieve the same goal. Third, to ensure a minimum level of proficiency in grants management, some agencies established grants management certification programs and tailored the certifications to fit the different roles within the grant workforce. For example, State tailored separate certification programs after recognizing two distinct roles played by its employees who manage grants. These agencies' experiences have implications for COFAR's plans to develop government-wide training standards, including creating grants management competencies, delivering training for those competencies, and establishing certification standards.

_____ **United States Government Accountability Office**

Contents

Figures

Abbreviations

A/OPE	Office of the Procurement Executive
ACF	Administration for Children and Families
ASPR	Assistant Secretary for Preparedness and Response
CDC	Centers for Disease Control and Prevention
CFO	chief financial officer
CLO	chief learning officer
CMS	Centers for Medicare & Medicaid Services
COFAR	Council on Financial Assistance Reform
DOT	Department of Transportation
Education	Department of Education
FAA	Federal Aviation Administration
FHWA	Federal Highway Administration
FMCSA	Federal Motor Carrier Safety Administration
GOR	grants officer representative
GPC	Grants Policy Committee
HHS	Department of Health and Human Services
HRSA	Health Resources and Services Administration
IDP	individual development plan
Leading EDGE	Leading Executives Driving Government Excellence
NHTSA	National Highway Traffic Safety Administration
NIH	National Institutes of Health
OMB	Office of Management and Budget
OPM	Office of Personnel Management
State	Department of State

GAO

U.S. GOVERNMENT ACCOUNTABILITY OFFICE

441 G St. N.W.
Washington, DC 20548

June 28, 2013

The Honorable Darrel Issa
Chairman
The Honorable Elijah E. Cummings
Ranking Member
Committee on Oversight and Government Reform
United States House of Representatives

The Honorable Thomas R. Carper
Chairman
The Honorable Tom Coburn, M.D.
Ranking Member
Committee on Homeland Security and Governmental Affairs
United States Senate

The Honorable Claire McCaskill
Chairman
Subcommittee on Financial and Contracting Oversight
Committee on Homeland Security and Governmental Affairs
United States Senate

Grants are a key tool used by the federal government to achieve a wide variety of national objectives such as providing medical, financial, housing, and foreign assistance, as well as constructing and maintaining our nation's highways, bridges, and mass transit systems. Federal outlays for grants to state and local governments totaled approximately $545 billion in fiscal year 2012, comprising over 15 percent of all federal outlays.[1] The value of these grants has grown considerably over the years, rising from $91 billion in fiscal year 1980 (about $225 billion in fiscal year 2012 constant dollars)—a real, inflation-adjusted increase of more than 140 percent.

---

[1] For additional information on the role and funding levels of federal grants, see GAO, *Grants to State and Local Governments: An Overview of Federal Funding Levels and Selected Challenges*, GAO-12-1016 (Washington, D.C.: Sept. 25, 2012). The dollar value of federal grants to state and local governments cited above does not include grants to others such as nonprofit organizations, research institutions, individuals, or foreign governments. According to the Office of Management and Budget, federal grants to state and local governments represent roughly 80 percent of all federal grant funding.

Given the role federal grants play in achieving national objectives, as well as grants' considerable growth in value and complexity over the past three decades, it is important that the federal workforce that manages these grants has the necessary knowledge and skills to do its job. In this regard, the government's approach to another tool it uses to achieve goals—purchasing goods and services through federal contracts—provides an interesting contrast. In fiscal year 2012, the federal government spent approximately $28 billion more on grants to state and local governments than it did on federal acquisitions. Under federal acquisitions law, there are clear government-wide training requirements for the acquisitions workforce intended to help ensure its quality and effectiveness.[2] However, similar government-wide training requirements do not exist for the grant workforce.

In light of this, you asked us to examine how the federal government trains its grant workforce and what challenges, if any, exist.[3] In this report, we (1) describe the federal grant workforce at selected agencies and analyze the challenge of identifying the workforce government-wide and (2) examine selected good practices agencies use and challenges they face, if any, in training the grant workforce, and the potential implications of these practices and challenges for a government-wide approach toward developing grants management competencies, training, and

---

[2] See the Office of Federal Procurement Policy Act, as amended (41 U.S.C. § 1703) and the Defense Acquisition Workforce Improvement Act (10 U.S.C. §§ 1741-46).

[3] For the purposes of this report, we defined the "grant workforce" as any federal personnel (not including contractors or grant recipients) whose official job responsibilities included administering or managing grants, either full time or part time, including any aspect of the grant life cycle. This could include administrative and fiscal functions, conducting audit work, as well as programmatic aspects of the grant. However, involvement in the grant work for these personnel needed to be consistent and not conducted on an *ad hoc* basis. We defined "training for the grant workforce" as making available to employees planned and coordinated educational programs of instruction in grants management related to the employee's job responsibilities. Such training could relate to a particular grant program or grants management in general. In addition, the training could be formal (such as classroom training, e-learning, or professional conferences that are educational or instructional in nature) or informal (such as participating in mentoring or developmental rotations).

certification. You were also interested in the federal acquisitions workforce, which we reported on separately.[4]

To accomplish our objectives, we gathered information both government-wide and at four specific agencies. To obtain a government-wide perspective, we reviewed federal employee data from the Office of Personnel Management's (OPM) online FedScope information system that supports statistical analyses of federal human resources data, administered a questionnaire to the chief learning officers (CLO) at 22 federal agencies with an active grant workforce, and reviewed documentation and interviewed officials from the Office of Management and Budget (OMB) and OPM.[5] To obtain illustrative examples of experiences, challenges, and good practices in training the grant workforce, we selected four agencies—the Departments of Education (Education), Health and Human Services (HHS), State (State), and Transportation (DOT). The four agencies we selected account for 84 percent of total grant dollars and 61 percent of total discrete grants awarded in fiscal year 2012. In addition, these agencies manage a variety of grant types, including formula, block, and project grants, and cover a broad range of areas including health, education, and transportation, among others.[6] To examine good practices that agencies use in training the grant workforce, we used criteria from our work on strategic training

---

[4] GAO, *Acquisition Workforce: Federal Agencies Obtain Training to Meet Requirements, but Have Limited Insight into Costs and Benefits of Training Investment*, GAO-13-231 (Washington, D.C.: Mar. 28, 2013).

[5] The 22 Chief Financial Officers (CFO) Act agencies with an active grant workforce at the time of this review were the Departments of Agriculture, Commerce, Defense, Education, Energy, Health and Human Services, Homeland Security, Housing and Urban Development, Interior, Justice, Labor, State, Transportation, Treasury, and Veterans Affairs; the Environmental Protection Agency; National Aeronautics and Space Administration; Nuclear Regulatory Commission; National Science Foundation; Small Business Administration; Social Security Administration; and the U.S. Agency for International Development. 31 U.S.C. § 901.

[6] The scope of this review is limited to grants and does not include cooperative agreements or other federal assistance.

and workforce planning in the federal government, internal control standards for training, and OPM guidance.[7]

To describe the federal grant workforce and analyze challenges related to workforce identification, we reviewed employee data from FedScope, collected workforce information through our 22-agency questionnaire and from our four case example agencies, and we reviewed documentation and interviewed knowledgeable officials at OMB, OPM, Education, HHS, State, and DOT. To describe how the federal grant workforce is trained and to identify challenges and good practices, we reviewed relevant federal laws and administrative guidance, collected information on training policies and practices in our questionnaire and in interviews with training officials at selected sub-agency components of our four case example agencies, and reviewed agency documents and collected information on training courses and their costs at Education, HHS, State, and DOT. To obtain information on government-wide policies and initiatives in this area, we reviewed documentation and interviewed officials at OMB and OPM. Since the focus of our work was on describing how the federal government trains its grant workforce, we conducted the individual agency reviews in order to identify illustrative examples of grants training experiences, challenges, and good practices and not to assess the specific grants training programs at these selected agencies. Additional details regarding our objectives, scope, and methodology are provided in appendix I. We include illustrative examples from our case example agencies throughout the report with additional details about grants training for each of the four case example agencies provided in appendix II.

We conducted this performance audit from May 2012 through June 2013 in accordance with generally accepted government auditing standards. Those standards require that we plan and perform the audit to obtain sufficient, appropriate evidence to provide a reasonable basis for our findings and conclusions based on our audit objectives. We believe that the evidence obtained provides a reasonable basis for our findings and conclusions based on our audit objectives.

---

[7] GAO, *Human Capital: A Guide for Assessing Strategic Training and Development Efforts in the Federal Government*, GAO-04-546G (Washington, D.C.: March 2004); GAO, *Human Capital: Key Principles for Effective Strategic Workforce Planning*, GAO-04-39 (Washington, D.C.: Dec. 11, 2003); and GAO, *Standards for Internal Control in the Federal Government*, GAO/AIMD-00-21.3.1 (Washington, D.C.: November 1999).

Background

There are no specific government-wide training standards or training requirements for the federal grant workforce; however, the administration has taken some steps toward developing such standards. Between 2004 and 2011, a work group within the administration's Grants Policy Committee (GPC) studied the issue of training and certifying the grant workforce, which led to a number of recommendations. However, the work group's recommendations were never formally adopted by the GPC. In 2011, OMB formed the Council on Financial Assistance Reform (COFAR), an interagency group of executive branch officials, to replace the GPC and another federal board—the Grants Executive Board—with the stated aim of creating a more streamlined and accountable structure to coordinate financial assistance, including grants. In November 2012, just over a year after it was created, COFAR identified the need to develop a qualified and professional workforce as one of five priorities to guide its work on grants management reform in the coming years. To accomplish this, COFAR set five goals:

- Establish core competencies for grants managers by September 2013.
- Develop a baseline body of knowledge as a shared resource by September 2013.
- Establish a government-wide resource repository for federal grants professionals by September 2013.
- Provide training for core competencies by September 2014.
- Establish certification standards by September 2015.

In developing proposals for grants training, COFAR considered the process and requirements that are in place for training the federal acquisitions workforce. Federal agencies generally do not need explicit statutory authority to make particular acquisitions of goods or services. However, for the procurement of goods and services, federal executive agencies are governed by a set of requirements specified in the Federal Acquisition Regulation. Congress has recognized the need for a professional acquisitions workforce by requiring executive agencies to establish management policies and procedures for the effective management of this workforce—including education, training, and career development.[8] Several governmental organizations play critical roles in assisting agencies to build and train their acquisitions workforce. These

---

[8] 41 U.S.C. § 1703 and 10 U.S.C. §§ 1741-46.

organizations include OMB's Office of Federal Procurement Policy, which provides government-wide guidance on managing the acquisitions workforce, and the Federal Acquisition Institute, which promotes the development of the civilian acquisitions workforce.[9]

In contrast to acquisitions, federal agencies do not have inherent authority to enter into grant agreements without affirmative authorizing legislation. Consequently, each federal grant program has legislation that identifies the types of activities that it can fund and the purposes it is to accomplish. Frequently, the authorizing legislation that establishes a particular grant program will define the program objectives and leave the administering agency to fill in the details through regulation. In addition to specific statutory requirements, OMB issues administrative requirements in the form of circulars. These circulars provide government-wide guidance that sets standards for a range of grants management activities, including grant application forms, cost principles, audits, and financial reporting. However, training is not one of the issues for which specific government-wide guidance is provided.

While many differences exist among grant programs, a basic distinction can be made between two broad grants management roles. The first role is **grants management specialist**—employees who generally possess detailed knowledge of OMB grants administration requirements, specific agency policies and procedures for grants management, and relevant laws and regulations to help ensure accountability of the grant funds. Grants management specialists are responsible for performing many of the daily grants management tasks from the pre-award phase through closeout.[10] The second role is **program specialist**—employees who possess expert knowledge in the specific area necessary to meet a

---

[9] While broad training requirements are set for the acquisition workforce in legislation (41 U.S.C. § 1703 and 10 U.S.C. §§ 1741-46), OMB establishes the government-wide training framework. See, for example, Office of Management and Budget, Policy Letter 05-01, April 15, 2005; and GAO-13-231.

[10] While there can be significant variation among different grant types, most competitive grants share a common life cycle for administering the grants: pre-award, award, implementation, and closeout. For additional information on the grant life cycle, see GAO-12-1016.

grant's goals.[11] Reflecting the wide variety of federal programs that grants support, individuals performing this role typically possess a specialized program or subject-matter expertise. These specialists can be involved in several stages of the grant process including announcing the terms and conditions of a grant, recommending potential grantees, and monitoring grantees' progress in achieving the grant's goals. Although these categories describe separate focus areas and many employees involved with grants concentrate on one or the other, the categories are not mutually exclusive. A single employee can carry out the functions typically associated with both a grants management specialist and a program specialist.

Identifying the Federal Grant Workforce Presents Challenges

Despite the existence of a "grants management specialist" job series, identifying the federal grant workforce presents challenges due to differences in how agencies manage grants and the range of employees involved in grants management. We have previously reported that organizations need to determine the workforce skills necessary to achieve their strategic goals as part of an effective training and development program.[12] However, identifying these skills, as well as the roles, responsibilities, and training needs of individuals in the federal grant workforce at a government-wide level remains a challenge. This is due to the different ways agencies assign grants management responsibilities to grants management specialists and program specialists and the wide range of job series the agencies use.

---

[11] For the purposes of this report, we refer to program specialists as those staff with specific expertise in the grant program and grants management specialists as those individuals with only grants management duties. Program specialists may be referred to by some agencies as "project officers," "program officers," or "grants officer representatives." Grants management specialists may also be referred to by some agencies as "grants officers."

[12] GAO-04-546G and GAO-04-39.

Agency Adoption of OPM's Grants Management Specialist Job Series Has Been Uneven Partly Due to Differences in How Agencies Manage Grants

Prior to 2010, no specific job classification existed for the many federal employees responsible for carrying out managerial and administrative tasks related to grants, including ensuring compliance with OMB and agency policies and procedures. In the absence of a specific job classification, officials at selected agencies told us that they classified these employees under a variety of other job series that did not focus on grants, such as general, administrative, and subject-matter job titles. OPM recognized the need for a classification that would more accurately capture the work of federal employees who manage grants, and in November 2010 the agency established a "grants management specialist" (series 1109). Since then, the extent to which agencies have adopted the 1109 job series has varied greatly. As of December 2012, there were 1,414 federal employees in the 1109 series in the 22 grant-making agencies we included in our survey.[13] More than half of these employees worked at HHS. In contrast, 5 of these agencies do not have any series 1109 employees and an additional 7 have fewer than 20 (see figure 1).

---

[13] In addition to the 1,414 employees in the 1109 series at the 22 CFO Act agencies with an active grant workforce at the time of our review, 45 employees at other federal agencies were also classified in the series.

Figure 1: Number of Grants Management Specialists (1109 Series) in 22 Grant-Making CFO Act Agencies

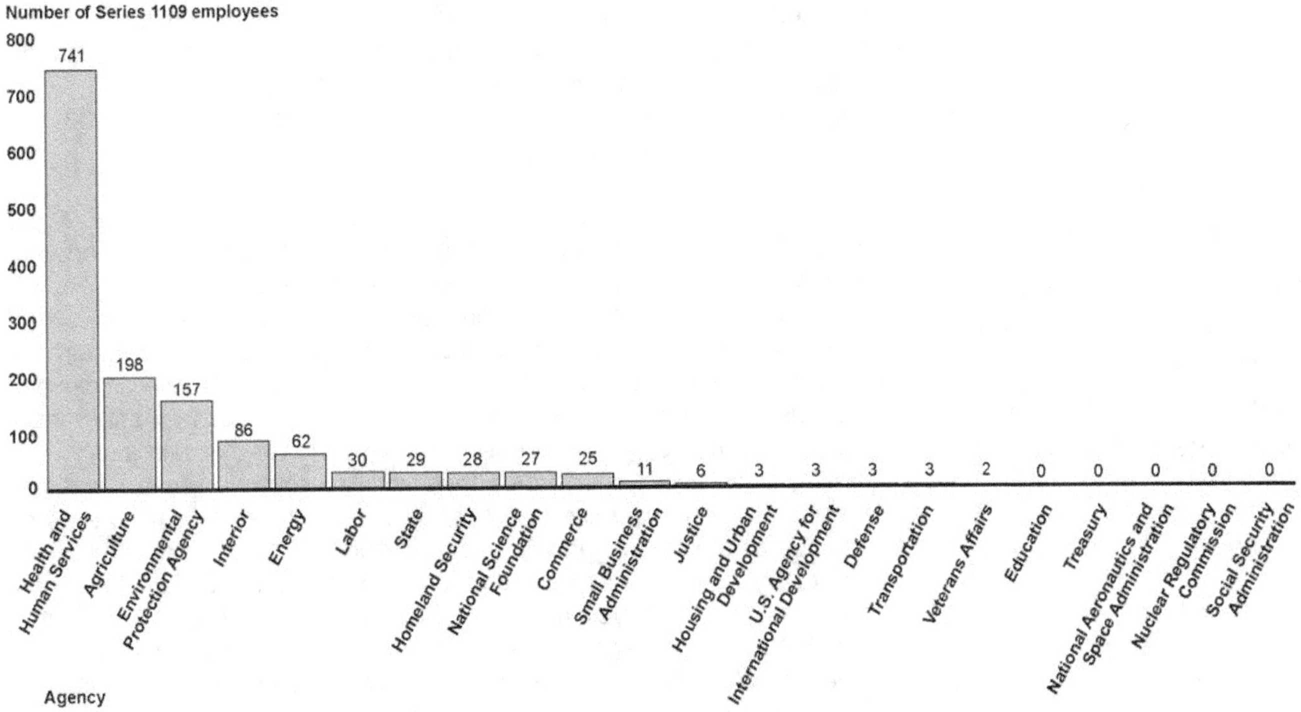

Number of Series 1109 employees

Source: GAO analysis of Fedscope data.

N = 1,414.

Note: Data reflect numbers of employees as of December 2012, the latest data available at the time of publication, for the 22 Chief Financial Officer (CFO) Act agencies with an active grant workforce during this review.

The way that an agency manages grants may explain whether, and to what extent, it has adopted the grants management specialist job series 1109. In the four agencies we selected for further review, we saw differences in the extent to which they adopted the 1109 series, partly because of different grants management approaches. At HHS, where grants management specialists work alongside program specialists, officials told us that they embraced the 1109 job series. Shortly after OPM introduced the series, HHS began moving hundreds of employees, who were classified in several general or miscellaneous administrative series and whose primary work responsibilities focused on carrying out managerial and administrative tasks, to the new 1109 series. In contrast, both Education and DOT—where program specialists primarily manage grants—largely chose not to use the new series. Officials at these agencies told us that this decision resulted from their grants management approach where program specialists, who have expert subject-matter knowledge in the grant program area, also carry out the functions of grants management specialists. These officials also had concerns about transitioning program specialists such as engineers or educational specialists, who have specific educational requirements, to the 1109 series which has no such requirements.

Agencies Assign Employees in a Wide Variety of Job Series to Manage Grants Other than the Grants Management Specialist Job Series

In addition to the 1109 grants management specialist series, the federal grant workforce includes a wide range of employees in other job series, many of whom function as program specialists. These employees generally possess specialized education and expertise in an area directly relevant to the grant's subject area. For example, at DOT, the employees responsible for managing federal airport safety and improvement grants are typically civil engineers (series 810), who are familiar with airport runway construction standards. Similarly, HHS employs social scientists (series 101) with expertise in child and family services as well as doctors and nurses (series 602 and 610, respectively) to manage and support grants that fund health care and related services to needy families. Some agencies, like DOT, typically rely upon program specialists to carry out both the grants management and program specialist functions, while others, such as HHS, employ individuals whose primary responsibility is to administer daily grants management tasks while working alongside program specialists.

With such a diverse range of job series across federal grant-making agencies and given the considerable variation in how agencies assign individuals to grants management roles, it is difficult to identify all the staff responsible for managing federal grants other than on an agency-by-agency basis. We asked the four agencies we focused on in this review—Education, HHS, State, and DOT—to identify the number of employees they considered to be in their grant workforce and provide us with breakdowns by job series. They identified over 5,100 employees, spanning more than 50 different occupational job series.[14] These include

---

[14] These employees represented staff whose official job responsibilities include administering or managing grants either full-time or part-time, including those personnel involved in any aspect of the grant life cycle. Since our definition of "grant workforce" did not include employees who were involved with grants on an irregular or *ad hoc* basis, rather than as a regular part of their job duties, the actual number of staff with some involvement with grants is likely to be higher.

grants management specialists, program specialists (e.g., public health program specialists, education program specialists, civil engineers, transportation specialists, and Foreign Service officers), auditors, and financial managers, among others. See figure 2 for a visual representation of the relative frequency of more than 90 percent of these occupational job series. For a complete listing of these job series as well as the total number of employees in each, as identified by Education, HHS, State, and DOT, see appendix III.

Figure 2: Relative Frequency of Occupational Series Comprising the Grant Workforce in Education, HHS, State, and DOT

Source: GAO analysis of HHS, DOT, Education, and State data.

N = 4,708 employees.

Note: This figure depicts the relative frequency of each job series by the size of the word or phrase describing the job series title. Job titles that appear larger occurred more frequently than those that

GAO-13-591 Training the Federal Grant Workforce

appear smaller. The figure represents over 90 percent of the grant workforce identified by Education, HHS, State, and DOT. It does not include 37 job series where fewer than 50 employees were identified because they were too small to be legible; this accounts for a total of 417 employees. The data reflect agency counts taken between December 2012 and June 2013.

With the exception of the grants management specialists in the 1109 series, grant officials at each of these four agencies told us that only a subset of those in the 57 job series they identified as part of the grant workforce are actually assigned to work on grants. The program specialists, accountants, contracting officers, and other individuals identified as part of the grant workforce generally comprised a relatively small subset of the total number of agency employees in those associated job series. For instance, while HHS employed over 6,800 doctors as medical officers (series 602) as of December 2012, officials identified only 29 of these as part of the grant workforce. Moreover, for some of the employees identified as being in the grant workforce, working on grants-related activities may only be part of what they do.

On a government-wide level, OMB staff told us that they understand that the 1109 series does not encompass the entire federal grant workforce. In a town hall meeting held in December 2012 with grant-making agencies to discuss COFAR priorities, COFAR officials recognized that government-wide efforts to develop training and certification standards will need to consider how to reach members of the grant workforce who are not in the 1109 series. To date, COFAR has not made public specific plans on how it will define the grant workforce, nor which members of the grant workforce—such as grants management specialists and program specialists—it intends to include when developing government-wide training standards.

Agency Practices in Support of the Grant Workforce Included Identifying Competencies, Providing Agency-Specific Training, and Using Certification Programs

Government-wide Grants Management Competencies Do Not Include Competencies for Program Specialists That Some Agencies Incorporated in Their Own Models

We previously reported on the value of identifying competencies that are critical to successfully achieving agency missions and goals, such as those related to grant making, and assessing gaps in those competencies among the workforce.[15] Competencies describe measurable patterns of knowledge, skills, abilities, behaviors, and other characteristics that an individual needs to perform work roles or occupational functions successfully. Understood another way, competencies specify what the person needs to do the job successfully. While there are other ways to identify training needs, such as through individual development plans or needs assessments, grants management competency models can be used to establish an overall framework to guide agencies' training efforts as well as to provide a basis for agencies to identify critical skills gaps in the workforce and training to address these gaps.

There have been previous efforts to develop government-wide grants management competencies, and another is planned by COFAR for 2013. These efforts date back to 2004 when the Chief Financial Officers Council's now defunct GPC formed a work group on training and certifying the grant workforce which, according to officials in this group, developed an initial draft set of competencies. However, after holding discussions with OPM, the work group decided not to pursue this effort because OPM decided to take on the task. Subsequently, in 2009, OPM released a government-wide grants management competency model.

---

[15] GAO-04-546G and GAO-04-39.

According to OPM officials who were involved in the effort, the model describes functional competencies that apply across multiple job series or occupations, similar to OPM's crosscutting leadership competencies.[16] In addition to numerous general competencies, the model identified five technical competencies specific to grants management (see table 1).[17] See appendix IV for the full set of OPM's grants management competencies. OPM's model has served as a framework to support a government-wide effort to assess critical skills gaps among the federal workforce. Through that effort, the administration identified seven mission critical competencies, and three were related to grants management. OPM officials told us that they are consulting with OMB staff and COFAR officials to determine a strategy for assessing skills gaps in these competencies.

Table 1: OPM's Technical Competencies for Grants Management

Compliance	Knowledge of procedures for assessing, evaluating, and monitoring programs or projects for compliance with federal laws, regulations, and OMB circulars
Financial Analysis	Knowledge of financial methods, procedures, and practices to assess the financial stability of those applying for, or receiving, federal grants or agreements
Financial Assistance Mechanisms	Knowledge of the differences between acquisition and financial assistance purposes and requirements; knowledge of federal assistance instruments, techniques, and procedures for grants (for example, block, mandatory, discretionary) and agreements (for example, cooperative, interagency)
Grants Management	Knowledge of requirements, practices, and procedures for soliciting, receiving, reviewing, and processing proposals, and awarding and administering grants and agreements
Grants Management Laws, Regulations, and Guidelines	Knowledge of principles, laws, regulations, policies, practices, and guidelines (for example, executive orders, Code of Federal Regulations, OMB circulars) of grant or agreement programs, including their order of precedence

Source: OPM.

[16] OPM's leadership competencies were developed as a guide for selecting strong leaders to serve in the Senior Executive Service and assessing executive experience and potential. The five Executive Core Qualifications—leading change, leading people, results driven, business acumen, and building coalitions—have a total of 28 executive competencies that underlie them.

[17] Competencies can be classified as general or technical. General competencies reflect the cognitive and social capabilities (e.g., problem solving, interpersonal skills) required for job performance in a variety of occupations. On the other hand, technical competencies are more specific as they are tailored to the particular knowledge and skill requirements necessary for a specific job.

Following the release of OPM's grants management competencies in 2009 not all grant-making agencies have embraced them. In response to our survey, half of agency CLOs (11 of 22) reported using the OPM competencies for purposes of identifying or developing grants training. The agency experiences described below may provide some insight into why some agencies have not used OPM's competencies and also raise questions about the sufficiency of OPM's competencies in meeting the needs of program specialists.[18]

At HHS, several grant-making operating divisions told us that while they found OPM's competency model useful for grants management specialists, they also needed a separate competency model for staff who function as program specialists working with their grants management specialists to manage grants. For example, officials in HHS's Health Resources and Services Administration (HRSA) noted that OPM's competencies were not appropriate for program specialists, so they developed a set of program specialist competencies. While these incorporate elements similar to OPM's technical competencies, they also include others that are more directly related to the employee's specific role in the HRSA grant program. HRSA highlights the role and authority of program specialists in the agency as distinct from that of the grants management specialist (series 1109 employees). In addition to competencies specifically related to grants management, HRSA also includes competencies related to policy analysis, research and evaluation, and technical assistance. For example, under the "policy analysis" competency, program specialists must be able to apply public health knowledge to HRSA's programs, perform policy analysis, and use this information to develop recommendations for improving HRSA programs or grantee performance. Under the "technical assistance" competency, program specialists need to be able to plan and conduct training and other activities that help grant applicants and grantees understand and comply with grant objectives and policies. In June 2013, the Centers for Disease Control and Prevention (CDC) finalized a set of competencies for program specialists which, like HRSA's program specialist competencies, includes competencies directly related to the employee's specific role in CDC grant programs.

---

[18] In June 2012, Leading EDGE, an interagency group composed of leaders from the Senior Executive Service, gathered to, among other things, look at the creation of grants competencies as one way to help develop and train career leaders and improve mission performance.

At Education, an official told us that OPM's single overarching grants management competency model did not fit the agency's culture or the way it managed grants. Unlike HHS, Education employs program specialists to manage grants through the entire process. Of the six job series under which the grant workforce is classified, five are mission critical occupations and the agency incorporates grants management competencies into the competency models for these occupations. For example, competencies for management and program analysts (series 343) include elements similar to the five OPM technical competencies. Education also includes competencies demonstrating leadership in the field and programmatic understanding and knowledge as well as technical assistance for both management and program analysts and education research analysts/education program specialists (series 1730/1720). An Education official explained that the agency's culture was resistant to a single, one-size-fits-all approach, and that staff were concerned that such a model would not adequately account for the technical and programmatic expertise needed to achieve program goals. Education used these grants management competencies as part of an agency-wide competency gap assessment, and is using the results to develop training to close these gaps.

A recent effort to develop government-wide grants management competencies provides further confirmation of the importance of developing competencies based on how agencies manage grants. In June 2012, senior executives from across the federal government gathered at the first meeting of the group Leading Executives Driving Government Excellence (Leading EDGE) to examine a variety of government-wide management issues and one issue the group selected to address was grants training. In November of that year, the group issued a report recommending a set of grants management competencies. The Leading EDGE report recognized that federal agencies target and structure their grants training depending on *how* they manage grants and that this varied across agencies. Further, the report acknowledged that some agencies assign grants management specialists to work in conjunction with program specialists while others assign an individual to perform both of these roles, and that grants training competencies needed to account for this variation.

Despite its recognition of the importance of considering the different ways that agencies manage grants when formulating a grants management competency model, the competency model the Leading EDGE report proposes is not significantly different from the model developed by OPM in 2009. In fact, the Leading EDGE model consists of the same competencies, defined in the same way, as those in OPM's model. The only change to the competencies is how Leading EDGE categorizes two competencies—"planning and evaluation" and "project management." In the OPM model these are listed as "general" competencies, whereas under the Leading Edge proposal, they become "technical" competencies. The Leading EDGE report does not specifically explain how making such a change would provide a meaningful alternative to the status quo that led agencies like HRSA and Education to explore other approaches. This is particularly true in light of the fact that, according to OPM officials, it is not uncommon for agencies to reclassify competencies as appropriate for their needs under existing competency models. So, while the Leading EDGE report represents a useful step forward in its recognition of the need to more fully integrate considerations related to program specialists when thinking about grants management competencies, its proposal, much like the current OPM model itself, is not likely to sufficiently address the need for competencies that are more responsive to the program specialist role.

We believe that these agency experiences, and that of Leading EDGE, provide important information for COFAR's consideration when developing government-wide grants management competencies. According to planning documents, COFAR expects to produce government-wide grants management competencies by September 2013. Toward this end, OMB staff told us that they have held three town hall meetings with agency officials between August 2012 and April 2013 in order to review COFAR's priorities, such as developing grants management competencies, and to obtain feedback from all federal grant-making agencies on what COFAR should consider as it moves forward on its priorities. Also, they engaged other stakeholders such as professional grants associations at meetings, conferences, and on conference calls. In addition, OMB staff said that COFAR plans to build on Leading EDGE's work as it develops new grants management competencies for the federal workforce.

Agencies Have Adapted Grants Training Courses and Developed Other Training Mechanisms to Address Agency-Specific Policies and Procedures

We have previously reported that agencies need to provide their workforce with training and development that is aligned with their missions, goals, and cultures.[19] We found that agencies provide formal and informal grants training through classroom instruction, online webinars, and meetings or briefings. The source of this training was generally a combination of direct agency provision and external vendors. According to our agency CLO survey, 7 of 22 agency CLOs responded that all or most of their grants training was provided by their agency. In addition, 9 of the 22 agency CLOs said they receive all or most of their grants training from commercial or non-profit sources, and the most common commercial provider by far was a single vendor. This vendor offers a set of core grants management courses designed to provide general knowledge that can be applied across the federal grants environment. Among these is an introductory course on grants as well as courses on cost principles, administrative requirements, and grants monitoring.

Agencies also reported difficulties finding grants training that met all of the needs of their grant workforce. Specifically, 13 of 22 agency CLOs responding to our survey said that they found the availability of training that met agency needs was at least a moderate challenge in training the grant workforce. For example, an agency said it was challenging to find courses that include instruction on specific statutes that authorize grant programs. In addition, in our interviews at selected agencies, officials told us that while external training courses were often useful in providing staff with general grants management knowledge, it was challenging to find courses that addressed agency or program-specific policies and procedures.

Of the four agencies we selected for a more detailed review, some responded to this challenge by customizing or supplementing foundational grants training courses provided by a commercial vendor or by developing training mechanisms, other than formal courses, for distributing agency-specific guidance to employees. For example, Education worked with a commercial vendor to tailor the vendor's grants training courses to reflect Education's policies and procedures and include examples and exercises specific to the agency. Although these courses were taught by the vendor's instructors, Education provided

---

[19] GAO-04-546G.

subject-matter experts to guide the customization of the courses to include agency policies and procedures. According to Education officials, the decision to tailor these external courses was based on participant feedback as well as their understanding of how adults process information while learning. The agency offered the courses to one cohort of employees in fiscal year 2011, to another cohort in fiscal year 2012, and to two cohorts in fiscal year 2013. Each cohort consisted of 35 employees.

In contrast, at HHS, officials chose to supplement commercially available grants training courses by developing their own grants training courses. For example, in addition to offering program specialists a core of vendor-provided courses, during the course of this review HRSA began requiring these employees to take three courses that the operating division specifically developed for its own grant policies and procedures. HRSA officials told us that while they found the commercial courses offered beneficial foundational knowledge on grants management, the courses did not fully address how the grants process operated at HRSA. For example, although the commercial courses cover administrative requirements for grants management as set by OMB, a goal of the HRSA program specialist training is to help program specialists understand how HHS policy relates to OMB guidance. The program specialist course manual uses practice scenarios with specific HRSA examples to present the reasoning behind when and which policies should supersede others. HRSA officials told us that the program specialist training was developed, in part, with the goal of improving customer service to grantees by ensuring that staff receive specific training on how to manage HRSA grants.

Each of the agencies that we selected for a detailed review also used other approaches to impart agency-specific guidance on grant policies and procedures to the grant workforce. For example, State used a number of training mechanisms in addition to formal courses to train its grant workforce both domestically and overseas. These included informal training sessions and a variety of online information sharing. Informal training included roundtable discussions facilitated quarterly by State's central grant policy office. These discussions allowed employees to share knowledge and perspectives with their peers on topics such as monitoring grant programs through site visits. State has several methods for sharing information, including an online platform where employees can find the latest information on policy guidance and regulations, grant reports, and grant systems as well as online repositories for frequently asked questions on agency grants policy and financial management of grants.

State officials told us that because OMB administrative guidance generally does not apply to the overseas grant environment, the agency has developed training for the grant workforce on agency-specific policies and procedures.[20] Using the training mechanisms described above, among other training methods, agency officials said they were able to provide employees with agency-specific training as issues arose and, through the use of online information sharing, easily reach those in the overseas bureaus.

On a government-wide level, COFAR plans to provide training on grants management core competencies by September 2014. Toward that end, OMB staff told us that COFAR has solicited feedback in town hall meetings with grant-making agencies, explored potential options for training venues, and is having HHS take the lead for COFAR in this effort.

Agency Experiences with Establishing Grants Management Certification Programs Illustrate the Usefulness of Tailoring Certification to Fit Roles and Responsibilities and the Value of Leadership Commitment

Certification programs are designed to ensure that individuals attain the knowledge and skills required to perform in a particular occupation or role by establishing consistent standards. Requirements for certification often include some amount of professional experience, continuing education, and successful completion of an assessment process that measures an individual's mastery of knowledge and skills against a set of standards.[21] Internal control standards for agencies state that management should identify the appropriate knowledge and skills, provide training, and establish a mechanism to help ensure that all employees receive appropriate training as part of establishing a control environment.[22] One internal control mechanism agencies have used is to develop certification programs to help ensure that staff demonstrate a level of competence in a particular field critical to the agencies' missions and goals.

---

[20] OMB circulars provide guidance for grants issued to educational institutions, state and local governments, and non-profit organizations. While one OMB circular does state that agencies may apply administrative guidance to foreign governments and organizations, other circulars do not offer specific guidance for grantees that are foreign governments or organizations.

[21] This definition is based on 2008 guidance from OPM. Professional certifications result in a credential issued by a third party. For example, the National Grants Management Association issues the Certified Grants Management Specialist credential. In contrast, the agency-issued certifications at two agencies we selected for detailed review—State and HHS—did not result in a third-party credential.

[22] GAO/AIMD-00-21.3.1.

Although not required government-wide, many agencies require or recommend grants management certifications in order to help ensure sound management practices across the agencies' grant workforce. Twenty-three percent (5 of 22) of agency CLOs responding to our survey reported that their agency requires some type of grants management certification and 73 percent (16 of 22) either require or recommend certification. The 16 agencies that either require or recommend grants management certification most often chose the following as one of the top three reasons why they do so:

- to ensure compliance with grants management regulations (15 of 16 agencies);
- to ensure accountability of grant funds (12 of 16 agencies); and
- to ensure uniform knowledge (11 of 16 agencies).

The experiences of agencies that have established certification programs suggest some broader lessons for establishing grants management certification standards government-wide that apply to the entire grant workforce. Two of the four agencies we selected for a more detailed review—State and HHS—have developed certification programs. State has implemented certification programs for all grants officers and, as of January 2013, for all grants officer representatives. To earn the grants officer certification employees must complete grants training, possess specific levels of education or experience, and comply with a continuing education requirement. To earn the grants officer representative certification employees must complete specific grants training and comply with a continuing education requirement. HHS developed an agency-wide certification program for grants management specialists, but only some of its operating divisions have implemented it. The certification program has four levels for grants management specialists, each of which requires staff to either complete specific training or to obtain an increasing amount of on-the-job experience. Several operating divisions also require that program specialists take some grants training, and one operating division is proposing a separate required certification program for program specialists.

One lesson that agency experiences suggest is the importance of clearly defining the roles and responsibilities of a diverse grant workforce and then appropriately tailoring certification standards in order to ensure that all key personnel in the grant workforce have appropriate and consistent knowledge to fulfill their roles. For example, State identified two key roles in its grants management process—grants officers and grants officer representatives—and tailored separate certifications for these roles.

Certified grants officers (e.g., grants management specialists) issue federal grant awards up to a specified value depending on the level of certification. As the value of grant awards increases, the amount of training required for the certification also increases. All levels of grants officer certification require completion of a certain number of training hours every 3 years in order to renew the certification. Grants officer representatives are program specialists who oversee the programmatic and technical aspects of the grant. They are appointed by grants officers and must complete two grants management courses before obtaining the grants officer representative certification. All grants officer representatives must update their training with additional grants training every 3 years. In 2007, we reported that State had inconsistent training and skills requirements for the grant workforce, and that State officials were concerned about the agency's ability to effectively manage its grants and other foreign assistance.[23] Agency officials told us that the grants officer representative certification was implemented in January 2013, to address inconsistencies in training for grants officer representatives across the agency.

In another example, HHS's guidance on its agency-wide certification program recognizes the important role that program specialists play in the technical, scientific, and programmatic aspects of grants. The guidance states that since program specialists work in partnership with grants management specialists, they should complete an orientation course in grants administration that emphasizes the program specialist's role in the grants management process. Completion of this orientation course in conjunction with joint nomination by the supervising program and grant officials results in certification as a program specialist. The guidance encourages program specialists to take further grants training, but does not require them to complete the grants management certification.

Another lesson illustrated by agency experiences in this area is the importance of ongoing leadership commitment and having a mechanism in place to track the implementation of training requirements. HHS developed an agency-wide professional certification program for the grant workforce in 1995, but the program was not fully implemented even though operating divisions were required to do so by guidance and an

---

[23] GAO, *Department of State: Human Capital Strategy Does Not Recognize Foreign Assistance Responsibilities,* GAO-07-1153 (Washington, D.C.: Sept. 28, 2007).

agency policy directive. We found that a limited number of grant-making operating divisions (4 of the 13) had taken action to implement the required certification program.[24] Grant officials in HHS's operating divisions told us that the program was inconsistently implemented because of changes in agency-level leadership and lack of enforcement. Other officials said that without enforcement of the certification requirement or updated agency-wide training guidance for grants management it was a challenge to obtain the resources needed and identify courses for training the grant workforce. Another potential factor contributing to uneven implementation was that HHS did not track most staff completion of the grants management certifications agency-wide, although operating divisions tracked staff completion where the requirement was enforced. Agency officials told us that they did track certification completion for those meeting the requirements of the highest certification level reserved for chief grants management officers, a position typically filled by members of the Senior Executive Service. According to these officials, the operating divisions at HHS nominate staff to receive the chief grants management officer certification and the agency-level grants policy division authorizes it. In contrast, State tracked whether staff completed requirements for its grants certifications in a database maintained by the Office of the Procurement Executive. Officials told us the system's visibility is a useful monitoring tool that encourages staff to complete the certification program in a timely manner.

We believe that the lessons from these two agencies that have developed certification programs provide important information for COFAR's consideration. On a government-wide level, COFAR has identified the need to ensure a consistent knowledge base and professionalize the grant workforce through developing certification standards by September 2015. OMB staff told us that they are looking into a multi-agency effort to develop a grants management certification that is being led by the Departments of Commerce and Energy. OMB staff also said they have had initial discussions on certification standards with professional grants associations.

---

[24] An official in one of these divisions told us that while they had taken steps to implement the certification requirement, they did not expect the requirement to be fully in place until the beginning of fiscal year 2014. While they don't have a grants management specialist certification, officials in an additional operating division told us that they are developing a certification program for program specialists that goes beyond the single course required in the HHS-wide guidance.

Conclusions

Given the importance of grants as a tool to achieve federal objectives and the large outlays the federal government makes to fund them each year, it is critical that the people who manage these grants—the federal grant workforce—be well-trained to handle their responsibilities. A key first step in this process is to have a clear understanding of the different ways agencies manage their grant processes and the wide variety of employees involved. A robust understanding of the diverse types of employees that make up the grant workforce and the key roles they carry out provides a foundation for the development of an effective government-wide grants training strategy.

In November 2012, COFAR identified the federal government's need to develop a qualified and professional grant workforce as one of its top priorities in the coming years. Toward that end, it announced a series of goals including the creation of government-wide grants competencies, training, and certification standards. As COFAR moves forward with plans to develop such standards, its efforts would benefit from considering the experiences of federal agencies in areas such as the development of grants management competencies and certification programs. Several agencies we reviewed found competencies to be a useful tool for structuring and identifying training needs. However, to fully support the agencies' grant-making missions and goals, the competencies need to address two key roles in the grant workforce: grants management specialists and program specialists. Although OPM's competency model appears to largely address the former, the experiences of agencies we reviewed suggest that the model was not directly applicable for program specialists involved in the grants process. Recognizing this gap, agencies took a variety of approaches including developing their own competency models for program specialists or finding ways to incorporate specific grants management competencies into existing competency models. Based on these agency experiences, future government-wide competencies that do not address the program specialist role will likely not be fully adopted by grant-making agencies.

Similar to agency experiences with competencies, some agencies have developed certification programs that have unique requirements depending on the role of the individual as either a grants management specialist or a program specialist. At one agency, for example, by developing a certification program that specifies a standard training curriculum and other requirements for both key roles in the grant workforce, the agency helped to ensure that key members of its grant workforce have appropriate levels of proficiency. Future government-wide certification standards that do not distinguish between the grants management specialist role and the program specialist role will likely not be fully adopted for the entire grant workforce by all grant-making agencies. As COFAR crafts government-wide standards for grants training, agency experiences highlight the importance of defining the roles of the grant workforce.

Recommendations for Executive Action

As COFAR works to professionalize the federal grant workforce, we recommend that the Director of OMB, in collaboration with COFAR, take the following two actions:

1. Include the program specialist role as COFAR develops a government-wide grants management competency model. This could be done by developing a separate model for program specialists or revising the existing grants management model so that it incorporates additional competencies for program specialists.

2. Distinguish between the grants management specialist role and the program specialist role as COFAR establishes government-wide certification standards for the federal grant workforce.

Agency Comments

We provided a draft of this report to the Secretaries of the Departments of Education, Health and Human Services, State, and Transportation; and to the Directors of the Office of Management and Budget and the Office of Personnel Management. OMB staff provided oral comments and concurred with our findings and recommendations. OMB staff, Education, HHS, and DOT also provided technical comments on the draft that we incorporated, as appropriate.

As agreed with your offices, unless you publicly announce the contents of this report earlier, we plan no further distribution until 30 days from the report date. At that time, we will send copies of this report to the Secretaries of the Departments of Education, Health and Human Services, State, and Transportation, and the Directors of the Office of Management and Budget and the Office of Personnel Management. In addition, the report will be available on our web site at http://www.gao.gov.

If you or your staff have any questions regarding this report, please contact me at (202) 512-6806 or by email at czerwinskis@gao.gov. Contact points for our Offices of Congressional Relations and Public

Affairs may be found on the last page of this report. GAO staff who made major contributions to this report are listed in appendix V.

Stanley J. Czerwinski
Director
Strategic Issues

Appendix I: Objectives, Scope, and Methodology

In order to better understand how the federal workforce responsible for managing grants is trained, and what challenges and good practices exist, we (1) described the federal grant workforce at selected agencies and analyzed the challenge of identifying the workforce government-wide; and (2) examined selected good practices agencies used and challenges, if any, they faced in training the grant workforce, as well as potential implications of these practices and challenges for government-wide efforts to develop grants training standards.

To obtain a broad view of how the grant workforce is trained government-wide, we reviewed relevant federal laws and administrative guidance and conducted a survey of chief learning officers (CLO) at the 24 Chief Financial Officers (CFO) Act agencies. The survey questionnaire included questions on grants-specific training, certification, administration and development of training, and challenges and good practices in training the grant workforce. Two agencies, the General Services Administration and the Office of Personnel Management (OPM), were dropped from our survey after officials in those agencies stated that they did not have any personnel actively working on grants. Each of the remaining 22 agencies responded to the survey, resulting in a 100 percent response rate from CFO Act agencies with an active grant workforce. The questionnaires were sent to the CLOs but they were asked to share them, as needed, with other knowledgeable agency staff in order to provide an informed response. Agencies were asked to return a single questionnaire that best represented their practices and challenges as a whole. Four agencies returned multiple questionnaires from sub-agency components. To address this, we developed a methodology for combining responses in order to formulate an agency-wide response. We also conducted follow-up conversations with agencies to clarify responses or collect additional details.

To obtain illustrative examples of experiences, challenges, and good practices in training the grant workforce, we conducted additional reviews at four agencies. We selected these agencies from among the 22 CFO Act agencies with an active grant workforce after considering the agencies' total grant obligations, number of grant programs, and number of discrete grants awarded (using fiscal year 2011 USASpending.gov data).[1] In addition, in making our selections we considered whether an agency had grants training or certification requirements, any good grants training practices as identified by its CLO, the existence of significant issues regarding grants or training as reported in our prior work, the number of grant-making operating divisions, the variety of grant types (formula, block, and project), major grant issue areas (such as health, education, and transportation) and functional areas (such as service delivery, construction, and research). The scope of this review was limited to federal grants and did not include cooperative agreements or other types of federal assistance. We selected agencies that administered a large majority of federal grant obligations and also collectively represented a range of positions on these other criteria. The four agencies we selected—the Departments of Education (Education), Health and Human Services (HHS), State (State), and Transportation (DOT)—account for over 84 percent of the federal government's total grant dollars obligated in fiscal year 2012, manage all three major grant types, and cover a broad range of grant issue areas. At each of these agencies, we reviewed documents including training materials and grants policy directives and interviewed training officials. We interviewed agency-level grants and training officials at each agency, and at the agencies we selected where grants training is generally managed at the sub-agency level—HHS, Education, and DOT—we also interviewed officials at selected sub-agencies. These sub-agency components were selected using criteria similar to that detailed above for agency selection. We also collected information on training courses, their costs, and the grant workforce at both the agency-level as well as all grant-making sub-agency components.

Since the focus of our work was to better understand and provide information on how the federal government trains its grant workforce, we conducted our reviews at each selected agency to identify examples of grants training experiences, challenges, and good practices, and not to audit their grants training programs. Accordingly, we did not seek to make an evaluative judgment of the specific grants training programs at the four selected agencies nor assess the prevalence of the practices or

---

[1] USASpending.gov was established by OMB to enhance the transparency of government expenditures. For grant awards, federal agencies report the amount of obligations they incur and information on the recipients of those awards in accordance with OMB guidance. For OMB guidance see: OMB, *Guidance on Data Submission under the Federal Funding Accountability and Transparency Act,* M-09-19 (Washington, D.C.: June 1, 2009).

challenges we cite either within or across the four agencies. Agencies and sub-agency components other than those cited for a particular practice may or may not also be engaged in the same practices. While the responses and comments provided on our survey reflect the views of the CLOs at 22 of the CFO Act agencies, the examples of good training practices and challenges we identified are from the four selected agencies and are therefore not generalizable to other agencies. To examine good practices that agencies use in training the grant workforce, we used criteria from our work on strategic training and workforce planning in the federal government, internal control standards for training, and OPM guidance.[2]

To describe the federal grant workforce and the challenge of identifying the workforce government-wide, we collected workforce data from the four case example agencies, reviewed data on the grants management specialist job series 1109, and interviewed officials at OPM. We requested data from our four case example agencies on the makeup of their grant workforce. To identify their grant workforce, cognizant grant officials at the agency or sub-agency component level generally made judgments regarding which employees to include and then used agency personnel databases to access job series data associated with those identified. To assess the reliability of these data, we examined the workforce data provided by the agencies for anomalies. This included obtaining data on the total number of federal employees in the 1109 grants management specialist series for each of the four selected agencies from FedScope.[3] We then compared the numbers of 1109 series employees reported by the agencies to the data in FedScope in order to confirm the data collected from the agencies for the 1109 series. Only minor differences in the total number of series 1109 employees were noted and this was expected due to the 4-month difference in the time frames covered by the data. We also interviewed officials at OPM to discuss the development of the 1109 job series for grants management

---

[2] GAO, *Human Capital: A Guide for Assessing Strategic Training and Development Efforts in the Federal Government*, GAO-04-546G (Washington, D.C.: March 2004); GAO, *Human Capital: Key Principles for Effective Strategic Workforce Planning*, GAO-04-39 (Washington, D.C.: Dec. 11, 2003); and GAO, *Internal Control and Management Tool*, GAO-01-1008G (Washington, D.C.: August 2001).

[3] FedScope is an OPM-sponsored, online information system that supports statistical analyses of federal human resources data. It can be accessed at http://www.fedscope.opm.gov/index.asp.

specialists and challenges associated with grant workforce identification. Based on our tests and discussions with agency officials, we determined that the data were sufficiently reliable for the purposes of this report. To obtain broad views on how the grant workforce is trained government-wide, we interviewed officials at the Office of Management and Budget and OPM. To understand the efforts of the Council on Financial Assistance Reform we reviewed documents produced by the Council and interviewed staff at OMB.

We conducted this performance audit from May 2012 through June 2013, in accordance with generally accepted government auditing standards. Those standards require that we plan and perform the audit to obtain sufficient, appropriate evidence to provide a reasonable basis for our findings and conclusions based on our audit objectives. We believe that the evidence obtained provides a reasonable basis for our findings and conclusions based on our audit objectives.

Appendix II: Overview of Grants Training at the Departments of Education, Health and Human Services, State, and Transportation

Department of Education

General Overview

The Department of Education (Education) is the third largest federal grant-making agency in total value of funding, administering approximately $44 billion in grants in fiscal year 2012. The agency administers formula, block, and project grants through eight program offices (see table 2). These grants support the nation's schools and students through programs such as Title I, Impact Aid, and Special Education.

Grants training is managed at both the agency- and program-office level. Program offices within Education have the option of setting training requirements for their grant workforce and grants training is required in three of the agency's eight grant-making program offices. Training requirements generally consist of several courses in grants management. On an agency-wide level, only one course is required; this course focuses on discretionary grant license holders. In addition to grants training courses, other related training opportunities offered by Education include informal brown bag sessions, mentoring, and on-the-job training.

Table 2: Department of Education Grant-Making Program Offices by Percent of Total Education Federal Funding for Grants in Fiscal Year 2012, Examples of Grant Programs, and Grants Training Requirements

Education grant-making program offices	Percent of total Education federal funding in grants FY2012[a]	Examples of grant programs	Grants training requirements (as set by the program office)[b]
Office of Elementary and Secondary Education	52%	Title I Grants to Local Educational Agencies; Impact Aid	Required training courses
Office of Special Education and Rehabilitative Services	36%	Special Education Grants to States; Rehabilitation Services	Training offered; no training requirements
Office of Postsecondary Education	5%	Higher Education Institutional Aid; International Research and Studies	Training offered; no training requirements
Office of Vocational and Adult Education	4%	Adult Education - Basic Grants to States; Career and Technical Education - National Programs	Training offered; no training requirements
Office of Innovation and Improvement	2%	Teacher Quality Partnership Grants; Charter Schools	Required training courses
Institute of Education Sciences	1%	Education Research, Development and Dissemination; Research in Special Education	Required training courses
Implementation and Support Unit	<1%	Race to the Top	Training offered; no training requirements

GAO-13-591 Training the Federal Grant Workforce

Appendix II: Overview of Grants Training at the
Departments of Education, Health and Human
Services, State, and Transportation

Education grant-making program offices	Percent of total Education federal funding in grants FY2012[a]	Examples of grant programs	Grants training requirements (as set by the program office)[b]
Office of English Language Acquisition	<1%	Foreign Language Assistance	No training requirements

Source: Funding data from USASpending.gov as of April 11, 2013; grant program titles collected from the Catalog of Federal Domestic Assistance; GAO analysis of Education data.

[a]Numbers may not add to 100 percent due to rounding.

[b]The agency-wide grants training requirement (one course for those holding discretionary grant licenses) is not included in this table. Grants training requirements in this table reflect what program offices set specifically for their grant workforce.

Grant Workforce

As of December 2012, Education officials estimated their total grant workforce to be approximately 761 employees, out of a total of more than 4,200 employees. The agency has no employees classified in the grants management specialist series because it uses program specialists to manage the entire grant process and because of essential job requirements of the six job series in which the program specialists are currently classified (see appendix III for a complete breakdown of the Education grant workforce by job series).

Selected Grants Management Training Practices

Grants Management Competencies and Assessing Training Needs

According to an Education official and agency documentation, the agency incorporates grants management competencies in the competency models for at least five of six job series which comprise the grant workforce. For example, technical competencies for management and program analysts (series 343) include proficiency in formula and discretionary grants and grant monitoring, as well as demonstrating programmatic understanding and knowledge.

Competencies are also used to identify training needs through a competency assessment for mission critical occupations; five of these occupations were positions that Education identified as being part of the grant workforce. For example, Education's fiscal year 2011 assessment determined that proficiency gaps existed in fiscal monitoring; policy, legislation, and administrative rulemaking; and audit-related competencies. The agency developed a strategy to close those gaps through formal classroom training as well as web-based training and informal seminars on the topics identified. A grants training official told us

Appendix II: Overview of Grants Training at the
Departments of Education, Health and Human
Services, State, and Transportation

that several of these courses are available and more are being developed to be offered in fiscal year 2013.

In addition to the agency-wide competency assessment, one program office, the Office of Elementary and Secondary Education, conducted its own learning needs analysis through a contractor in 2012. This analysis assessed the learning needs for two positions, one of which was a grants specialist. The assessment was conducted through a survey of non-supervisory staff within the program office, who were asked to indicate the importance of tasks or content knowledge to their day-to-day work and the type of professional development desired in the next year. As a result of this learning needs assessment, a program office official reported that data analysis courses were procured to support professional development among staff members. This official also told us that while the Office of Elementary and Secondary Education plans to contract for a learning needs assessment every 3 years, they also have developed a tool for managers and staff to use annually in between external assessments in order to help grants specialists prepare their individual development plans.

Grants Training

The agency requires one grants training course agency-wide; this annual one-hour briefing is intended for those employees holding a discretionary grant license, which allows them to obligate and award grant funds. According to an Education official, the annual briefing is designed to provide license holders an update on legislative and regulatory developments that impact the agency's grants administration policies. The briefing also offers license holders an opportunity to share best practices, common concerns, and recommendations on how to improve the grants process.

In another agency-wide effort, according to agency officials, Education worked with a commercial vendor in 2010 to develop and customize a curriculum of eight grants management courses that lead to a grants management training certificate. Topics covered by the courses include grants monitoring, cost principles, administrative requirements, and accountability. These courses are offered to cohorts of 35 employees and each of the agency's program offices receives a certain number of slots in each cohort. Given criteria from the central learning and development office, it is the responsibility of the program offices to determine which of their employees are substantially involved in grants administration and management and would most benefit from the grants management curriculum. By offering the eight courses to cohorts of employees,

Appendix II: Overview of Grants Training at the
Departments of Education, Health and Human
Services, State, and Transportation

Education officials told us that they saved over $64,000 per cohort, or 31 percent of the cost to provide the courses to 35 employees individually in fiscal year 2013.

As reported by officials in each grant-making program office, 3 of 8 program offices at Education require grants training and 7 of 8 do offer grants training courses or other training opportunities to the grant workforce. For example, the Office of Innovation and Improvement offers an on-boarding program for new staff that includes courses on grants management and grants monitoring. In addition to these courses, this office holds internal brown bag sessions and a speaker series to address grant issues.

Certification

According to agency officials, Education does not require a grants management certification. Although it does offer training that leads to a grants management certificate, it does not offer a grants management certification program for its grant workforce.

Other Practices

Officials in Education's program offices, as well as officials in the centralized offices that offer training, told us that to evaluate Education's grants training courses offered in fiscal years 2011 and 2012 they collected information on participant satisfaction for a majority of the courses offered. Many officials did not respond or did not know if they collected information for other types of evaluation. However, those that did respond reported that they collected information on knowledge gained for more than half of courses offered and did not collect information on the impact on individual behavior or return on investment for any courses offered.

Education officials said they plan to begin collecting information on the impact of the commercial vendor-provided courses that make up their grants management training certificate on individual and organizational performance in the summer of 2013. To assess this training, Education expects to distribute a survey to training participants as well as their supervisors. Based on a prototype we obtained for review, the survey will ask about the extent to which training has been applied on the job as well as the courses' impacts on grants management performance and achieving organizational grants management goals.

In addition to measuring the impact of individual courses, Education officials told us that they measure the impact of training on performance through multi-year analysis of the results of the biennial mission critical occupations competency assessment. The assessment measures the

Appendix II: Overview of Grants Training at the
Departments of Education, Health and Human
Services, State, and Transportation

current and desired proficiency of employees in particular competencies and allows Education to target proficiency gaps for closure. According to these officials, assessment of proficiency gaps helps them to understand the developmental needs of the workforce and then provide training that targets these needs. By examining changes in workforce proficiencies over multiple years, Education hopes to assess the effectiveness of its training curricula.

Department of Health and Human Services

General Overview

HHS is the largest federal grant-making agency in terms of total federal grant funds, administering approximately $333 billion in grants during fiscal year 2012. Formula, block, and project grants are administered across 13 operating divisions within HHS (see table 3).[1] These grants support medical services and research including Medicaid, Temporary Assistance for Needy Families, Head Start, health centers, medical research, and preventive health services. Grants training is managed by the operating divisions, with general training standards and guidance offered through the Office of Grants and Acquisition Policy and Accountability's division of grants. Training in grants management is required for at least part of the grant workforce in 11 of 13 operating divisions, and these requirements range from a set of courses to professional development activities toward earning a certification in grants management.

---

[1] HHS officials told us that 10 operating divisions and three offices within the Immediate Office of the Secretary of Health and Human Services administer grants. For the purposes of this report, we refer to each of these 13 grant-making offices as operating divisions. Within the Immediate Office of the Secretary, the three offices that administer grants include the Office of the Assistant Secretary for Preparedness and Response, the Office of the Assistant Secretary for Health, and the Office of the National Coordinator for Health Information Technology.

Appendix II: Overview of Grants Training at the
Departments of Education, Health and Human
Services, State, and Transportation

Table 3: HHS Grant-Making Operating Divisions by Percent of Total HHS Federal Funding for Grants in Fiscal Year 2012, Examples of Grant Programs, and Grants Training and Certification Requirements

HHS grant-making operating division	Percent of total HHS federal funding in grants FY2012	Examples of grant programs	Grants training and certification[a]
Centers for Medicare & Medicaid Services	77%	Medicaid; Children's Health Insurance Program	Project grants: Required training courses[b] Formula grants (e.g., Medicaid): training offered[c]
Administration for Children and Families	14%	Temporary Assistance for Needy Families; Head Start	Required training courses and optional certification
National Institutes of Health	5%	Allergy, Immunology and Transplantation Research; Biomedical Research and Research Training	Required training courses and certification
Health Resources and Services Administration	2%	Health Center Program; HIV Care Formula Grants	Required training courses for program specialists. Required certification for program specialists expected to be implemented in fiscal year 2013
Substance Abuse and Mental Health Services Administration	<1%	Block Grants for Prevention and Treatment of Substance Abuse; Sober Truth on Preventing Underage Drinking Act	Training offered; no training requirements
Administration for Community Living	<1%	Special Programs for the Aging; Nutrition Services Incentive Program	Required training courses[b]
Immediate Office of the Secretary of Health and Human Services[d]	<1%	National Bioterrorism Hospital Preparedness Program; Pregnancy Assistance	Required training courses in one of the three grant-making offices[b]
Centers for Disease Control and Prevention	<1%	Preventive Health Services Sexually Transmitted Diseases Control Grants; Preventive Health and Health Services Block Grant	Required training courses[b]
Indian Health Service	<1%	Special Diabetes Program for Indians Diabetes Prevention and Treatment Projects; Demonstration Projects for Indian Health	Required training courses and certification
Agency for Healthcare Research and Quality	<1%	Research on Healthcare Costs, Quality and Outcomes; National Research Service Awards Health Services Research Training	Required training courses[b]
Food and Drug Administration	<1%	Food and Drug Administration Research	Training offered; no training requirements; required certification program expected to be implemented in fiscal year 2014

Source: Funding data from USASpending.gov as of April 11, 2013; grant program titles collected from the Catalog on Federal Domestic Assistance; GAO analysis of HHS data.

[a]Training courses required may not be mandatory for all members of the grant workforce. Unless otherwise indicated, training and certification is required for grants management specialists.

Appendix II: Overview of Grants Training at the
Departments of Education, Health and Human
Services, State, and Transportation

[b]Officials in these operating divisions told us that they require grants management specialists to complete a set of grants management courses. These same courses are also required as a key component of certification in the operating divisions that have implemented or proposed a certification program. CMS officials told us that, while they do not have a formal certification program in place for project grants, they consider this set of courses to meet the HHS-wide certification requirements. For the Immediate Office of the Secretary, the set of courses was only required in the Office of the National Coordinator for Health Information Technology

[c]CMS officials told us that they do not require grants training for Medicaid and other formula grants. They further explained that, because external vendors do not offer training that addresses what they viewed as the unique needs of Medicaid, CMS offers training on an as-needed basis. Most training occurs on-the-job, but can also include courses on topics such as financial management.

[d]Within the Immediate Office of the Secretary, three offices administer grants—the Office of the Assistant Secretary for Preparedness and Response, the Office of the Assistant Secretary for Health, and the Office of the National Coordinator for Health Information Technology.

Grant Workforce

HHS officials in each of the 13 operating divisions that administer grants, as well as officials in the agency's Division of Grants, estimated the total grant workforce to be approximately 2,166 employees, out of a total workforce of over 86,500. All HHS grant-making operating divisions have at least some employees classified in the grants management occupational series (1109). These grants management specialists work with program specialists to manage grants.

Selected Grants Management Training Practices

Grants Management Competencies and Assessing Training Needs

HHS does not have agency-wide competencies for the grant workforce, however several operating divisions at HHS reported having grants management competencies to support their training efforts. These competency models vary across each operating division. One operating division, the Centers for Medicare & Medicaid Services (CMS), reported applying OPM's grants management competency model directly, while several others had a subset of competencies similar to that included in OPM's model. Three agencies, the Health Resources and Services Administration (HRSA), the Centers for Disease Control and Prevention (CDC), and the Office of the Assistant Secretary for Preparedness and Response (ASPR) identified separate competency models for program specialists.

At HHS, officials in several operating divisions told us that they use both competencies and individual development plans or assessments to determine training needs. For example, HRSA conducted a training needs assessment that highlighted areas for additional training in grants management. Based on this and the identification of program specialists as being critical to the grants management process, HRSA developed a training program for program specialists that will support a certification requirement that officials expect to implement in fiscal year 2013. HRSA officials told us that they are working toward developing a similar program for grants management specialists.

Grants Training

According to agency officials, HHS does not require any agency-wide grants training, however, all operating divisions at HHS reported offering grants training to their grant workforce with 85 percent (11 of 13) of HHS operating divisions requiring some amount of training. Training courses offered include general grants management training courses that cover topics such as OMB circulars, cost principles, and monitoring. In addition, the National Institutes of Health (NIH) and HRSA have developed customized training specific to their operating divisions and grants. According to officials and documentation, NIH requires a month-long orientation to grants management and HRSA developed a three-course introduction to grants management. Several operating divisions offer informal training courses, webinars or other sessions to address current topics or specific issues. For example, the Administration for Children and Families (ACF) reported offering several informal courses including one on child welfare/child support and another on Temporary Assistance for Needy Families fiscal management.

Certification

While HHS developed policy and guidance that required agency-wide certification of its grant workforce in 1995, only four of its operating divisions have taken steps to implement it. Two of the 13 HHS operating divisions—NIH and the Indian Health Service—required grants management specialists to be certified in grants management, while ACF offers its certification program as an option to grants management specialists. Officials in the Food and Drug Administration have developed a proposal for a similar certification program and told us that they plan to implement it in fiscal year 2014. Each of these certification programs is based upon the agency-wide Grants Management Professional Development program established by HHS in 1995. This program was not widely enforced due to changes in leadership, but the requirement still resides in the agency's Grants Policy Directives and *Awarding Agency Grants Administration Manual*. In addition to these four certification programs for grants management specialists, HRSA is developing a required certification program for program specialists that will be fully implemented in fiscal year 2013. Once the program specialist certification is in place, HRSA officials told us that they plan to develop a similar certification for grants management specialists. Finally, five operating

Appendix II: Overview of Grants Training at the
Departments of Education, Health and Human
Services, State, and Transportation

divisions require their grants management specialists to complete a set of grants management courses from an external vendor, although they do not have the certification program in place. These same courses are an integral part of the certification program that the four operating divisions described above have implemented or proposed.

While the agency-wide certification program has not been fully implemented across all operating divisions, HHS officials told us that they have an agency-wide certification process in place for those meeting the requirements of the highest certification level—an operating division's chief grants management officer. In addition, in the years after the certification program was developed, officials told us that the agency provided grants training courses both internally through HHS University as well as through an external vendor to make grants training available to the operating divisions.

Other Practices

HHS operating divisions, as well as the agency's Division of Grants, reported that to evaluate their grants training courses offered in fiscal years 2011 and 2012 they

- collected information on participant satisfaction for a majority of the courses offered,
- collected information on knowledge gained in over half of the courses offered, and
- did not collect information on the impact on individual behavior or return on investment for any courses offered.

However, officials explained that while they understand that information gathered on participant satisfaction for courses taken by commercial vendors is available from the vendor for review, these results are typically not requested by the agency.

Appendix II: Overview of Grants Training at the
Departments of Education, Health and Human
Services, State, and Transportation

Department of State

General Overview

The Department of State (State) administered over $511 million in project grants in fiscal year 2012.[2] These grants fund a variety of assistance programs worldwide, including those supporting Democracy, Human Rights and Labor; Weapons Removal and Abatement; Professional, Cultural, and Educational Exchange Programs; Public Diplomacy Programs around the world including Iraq, Afghanistan, and Pakistan; Combating Human Trafficking; and Refugee Assistance, among others (see table 4).

At State, training of the grant workforce is managed at the agency level through the Office of the Procurement Executive (A/OPE). A/OPE sets training requirements for the grant workforce and collaborates with the Foreign Service Institute to help ensure that training courses are appropriately developed and delivered. Additional training on financial management of grants is developed by the Office of Federal Assistance Financial Management. Training and certification is required for all grants officers and grants officer representatives. While training for grants is centrally managed, each grant may be managed by a single or multiple bureaus depending on the type of assistance being provided. For instance, for grants that support a particular country or region, such as Iraq Assistance Programs, multiple bureaus may manage the funds to support a range of assistance programs. On the other hand, if the grant supports assistance in a particular program, such as educational exchanges, a single bureau, the Bureau of Educational and Cultural Affairs, may manage most or all of the funds.

---

[2] While the scope of this report excludes cooperative agreements, State administers over $823 million in cooperative agreements. Officials told us that the grant workforce that manages project grants is also responsible for managing cooperative agreements and receives the same training.

Appendix II: Overview of Grants Training at the
Departments of Education, Health and Human
Services, State, and Transportation

Table 4: Examples of Department of State Federal Funding for Grants in Fiscal Year 2012

Grant program	Total federal funding in grants FY2012	Percent of total federal funding in grants FY2012[a]
International Programs to Support Democracy, Human Rights and Labor	$134,919,683	26
Weapons Removal and Abatement	$101,689,374	20
Professional and Cultural Exchange Programs - Citizen Exchanges	$42,079,026	8
Public Diplomacy Programs for Afghanistan and Pakistan	$33,276,979	7
General Department of State Assistance	$33,154,221	6
Middle East Partnership Initiative	$19,484,689	4
Criminal Justice Systems	$18,815,930	3
East Asia and Pacific Grants Program	$17,197,277	3
International Programs to Combat Human Trafficking	$14,912,809	3
Public Diplomacy Programs	$12,920,058	3
EUR/ACE Humanitarian Assistance Program	$10,248,694	2
Overseas Refugee Assistance Programs for Africa	$7,704,597	2
Professional and Cultural Exchange Programs – Special Professional and Cultural Programs	$7,036,952	1
Counternarcotics	$6,890,530	1
Environmental and Scientific Partnerships and Programs	$6,788,996	1
Other	$44,259,514	9
Total	**$511,379,329**	

Source: Funding data from USASpending.gov as of April 11, 2013.

Note: Grants at State can be managed by multiple bureaus so we do not break down the grant funding by bureau.

[a]Numbers may not add to 100 percent due to rounding.

Grant Workforce

At State, agency policy states that grants are managed by warranted grants officers who are authorized to award grants up to a specified amount. Grants officers appoint grants officer representatives (GOR) to assist with technical and programmatic aspects of the grant. These two positions correspond to the grants management specialist and program specialist, respectively, as described in our report. In addition, financial management officers assist with fiscal management aspects of the grants process. State estimated that there are approximately 605 grants officers, most of whom are stationed overseas. In addition, 280 positions, including financial management officers, support those grants officers at overseas posts and in bureaus domestically. The GOR certification program was effective as of January 2013 and GORs had up to six

Appendix II: Overview of Grants Training at the
Departments of Education, Health and Human
Services, State, and Transportation

months to meet the certification requirements, thus State did not yet have a complete accounting of all certified GORs at the time of publication. A full accounting is expected by late summer 2013 when all GORs are required to be certified and registered in State's database that tracks both certified grants officers and GORs.

The grant workforce consists primarily of Foreign Service officers serving in posts around the world. State officials explained that, at these posts, not all Foreign Service officers work on grants, but those that do are responsible for multiple tasks, including managing grants. As a result, there are a lot of personnel that work on grants, and for many of the 740 Foreign Service officers identified as part of the grant workforce, grant-related tasks are a part-time responsibility.

Selected Grants Management Training Practices

Grants Management Competencies and Assessing Training Needs

State officials told us that, during the time of this review, they did not use grants management competencies for the purposes of identifying training. Beyond the required training and certification for grants officers and GORs, these officials explained that they assess any additional training needs as needed through management reviews. For instance, after review of grants administration at the Bureau of Educational and Cultural Affairs, it was determined that the grant workforce was lacking expertise in several areas. To address the specific training needs of the bureau's employees, A/OPE developed training for the bureau that augmented the formal training courses.

Grants Training

State requires all grants officers and GORs to complete training in grants management. Course topics include an introduction to grants and cooperative agreements, an introduction to monitoring grants, and ethics. As State officials explained, some of the required training courses were developed within the agency because the general training available from commercial vendors did not meet the needs of their staff. For example, most of State's grant recipients are foreign organizations, and the training from commercial vendors does not include specific grants management scenarios that staff are likely to encounter with foreign grant recipients. State officials told us that because OMB administrative guidance does not apply to the overseas grant environment the agency trains the grant workforce on agency-specific policies and procedures. After designing its own courses, State was also able to offer the course through a distance-

Appendix II: Overview of Grants Training at the
Departments of Education, Health and Human
Services, State, and Transportation

learning system that allowed grants officers and GORs overseas to access the training.

In addition to formal training courses, State offers informal training to its grant workforce through a variety of mechanisms. These include informal training sessions and a variety of online information sharing. For example, officials told us that, at quarterly meetings facilitated by State's central grants policy office, roundtable discussions allow employees to share knowledge and perspectives with their peers on topics such as monitoring grant programs through site visits. Officials told us that State has several methods for sharing information, including an online platform where employees can find the latest information on policy guidance and regulations, grant reports, and grant systems as well as online repositories for frequently asked questions on agency grants policy and financial management of grants.

Certification

As described in the agency's grants policy directives, State has implemented two certification programs—one for grants officers and the other for GORs. Both certifications require completion of specific grants training and have continuing education requirements. The grants officer certification also requires certain levels of education or experience. Certified grants officers are warranted to issue federal grant awards up to a specified value depending on the level of certification. As the value of grant award increases, the amount of training required for the certification also increases. All levels of grants officer certification require completion of a certain number of training hours every 3 years in order to renew the certification. GORs must complete two grants management courses before obtaining the grants officer representative certification. After certification the GOR is eligible to be designated to a specific agreement by the grants officers. In addition, all GORs must update their training with additional grants training every 3 years. The grants officer representative certification was implemented in January 2013 to help address inconsistencies in the level of training for grants officer representatives across the agency. Staff completion of both grants certification requirements is tracked in a database maintained by the Office of the Procurement Executive.

Other Practices

State officials reported that to evaluate grants training courses offered in fiscal years 2011 and 2012 they

- collected information on participant satisfaction for all four of the grants management courses offered,

Appendix II: Overview of Grants Training at the
Departments of Education, Health and Human
Services, State, and Transportation

- collected information on knowledge gained in one of these courses, and
- did not collect information on the impact on individual behavior or return on investment for any courses offered.

Officials indicated that the feedback they received from participants on commercial vendor courses is what prompted them to develop customized courses to reflect State grants management practices and scenarios.

Department of Transportation

General Overview

The Department of Transportation (DOT) is the second largest federal grant-making agency in total value of federal grant funds, administering approximately $52 billion in grants in fiscal year 2012. Formula and project grants are administered across 10 operating administrations within DOT (see table 5). These grants support the nation's highways, mass transit systems, railroads, and airports through programs such as Highway Planning and Construction and the Airport Improvement Program.

While the Financial Assistance Policy and Oversight Office issues agency-wide communications on general training requirements and works with OMB on government-wide training efforts, grants training is managed by the 10 grant-making operating administrations. The operating administrations have the option of setting grants training requirements, and requirements exist in 7 of the 10 operating administrations. These requirements range from a single course to a set of courses that lead to a grants management certificate. In addition to grants training courses required or offered, other training opportunities offered by operating administrations to address grant issues include online webinars, internal brown bags, working groups, and on-the-job training.

Appendix II: Overview of Grants Training at the
Departments of Education, Health and Human
Services, State, and Transportation

Table 5: DOT Grant-Making Operating Administrations by Percent of Total DOT Federal Funding for Grants in Fiscal Year 2012, Examples of Grant Programs, and Grants Training Requirements

DOT grant-making operating administration	Percent of total DOT federal funding in grants FY2012[a]	Examples of grant programs	Grants training requirements
Federal Highway Administration	68%	Highway Planning and Construction; Recreational Trails Program	Training offered; no training requirements
Federal Transit Administration	24%	Federal Transit Formula Grants; Federal Transit Capital Investment Grants	Required training courses
Federal Aviation Administration	6%	Airport Improvement Program; Aviation Research Grants	Required training courses[b]
National Highway Traffic Safety Administration	1%	State and Community Highway Safety; Alcohol Impaired Driving Countermeasures Incentive Grants	Training offered; no training requirements
Federal Motor Carrier Safety Administration	<1%	Border Enforcement Grants; Commercial Driver's License Program Improvement Grant	Required training courses
Pipeline and Hazardous Materials Safety Administration	<1%	Technical Assistance Grants; Pipeline Safety Program State Base Grant	Required training courses
Research and Innovative Technology Administration	<1%	University Transportation Centers Program; Biobased Transportation Research	Training offered; no training requirements
Federal Railroad Administration	<1%	High-Speed Rail Corridors and Intercity Passenger Rail Service—Capital Assistance Grants; Railroad Development	Required training course
Office of the Secretary	<1%	National Infrastructure Investments	Required training course
Maritime Administration[c]	0%	America's Marine Highway Grants	Required training courses

Source: Funding data from USASpending.gov as of April 11, 2013; grant program titles collected from the Catalog of Federal Domestic Assistance; GAO analysis of DOT data.

[a]Numbers may not add to 100 percent due to rounding.

[b]Grants training requirements only applicable for the Office of Airports within FAA. The Office of Airports manages a majority of FAA's grant funds.

[c]The Maritime Administration did not obligate grant funds in fiscal year 2012, according to USASpending.gov data as of April 11, 2013.

Grant Workforce

DOT officials in each of the 10 grant-making operating administrations estimated the total grant workforce to be approximately 1,313 employees and the total workforce at the agency is over 57,000 employees. The agency has only one employee classified in the 1109 grants management series because it employs program specialists to manage the entire grants process. However, in the course of our review, one operating administration, the Federal Motor Carrier Safety Administration (FMCSA), established a grants management office and hired employees in the 1109

**Appendix II: Overview of Grants Training at the
Departments of Education, Health and Human
Services, State, and Transportation**

grants management series to support this office. Program specialists at DOT are classified in more than 30 different job series (see appendix III for a complete breakdown of the DOT grant workforce by job series).

Selected Grants Management Training Practices

Grants Management Competencies and Assessing Training Needs

While DOT does not have agency-wide competencies for the grant workforce, operating administrations use other methods to identify training needs for the grant workforce. For example, officials at the Office of Airports in the Federal Aviation Administration (FAA) told us that they use the *FAA Human Resource Policy Manual* and a standardized job analysis tool to help supervisors identify and prioritize appropriate training for employees' individual development plans. In broader efforts to assess training needs, a Federal Transit Administration official told us that they have contracted with a private company to conduct a comprehensive training needs assessment and develop a 3-year plan to address the training needs. One operating administration, the National Highway Traffic Safety Administration (NHTSA), told us that they have draft grants management competencies that are scheduled for finalization by the end of fiscal year 2013. According to NHTSA officials, the competencies will be used to conduct periodic assessments, identify training needs, and develop individual development plans.

Grants Training

According to agency officials, DOT does not require any agency-wide grants training, however, all of the grant-making operating administrations at DOT offer grants training to their grant workforce and 70 percent (7 of 10) of the operating administrations require some amount of grants training. Training courses offered, according to operating administration officials, include general grants management training, such as courses on OMB circulars, costs principles, and monitoring, as well as customized training specific to the operating administrations' grant programs, including FMCSA's 3-day grants management manual training, the Federal Highway Administration's (FHWA) online training courses on planning and research grants, and the Office of Airports' 3-day course on airport financial assistance, provided by the FAA Academy. External vendors as well as the agency provide grants training at the operating administrations. Agency-provided grants training is developed by subject-matter experts within the operating administrations or by agency-affiliated training institutes. For example, for FHWA, the National Highway Institute has developed a series of web-based and classroom courses on planning and research grants. Topics covered in this series include common grant rules, grant administration, cost principles, and audits.

DOT employs program specialists to manage the entire grant process and, operating administrations provide training on both programmatic and technical aspects of grants as well as on general grants management. For example, officials at FAA's Office of Airports told us that their grant workforce needed highly specific technical and professional knowledge, skills, and abilities related to airport planning, engineering, construction, and operational and environmental matters. The Office of Airports used courses from the FAA Academy to provide training that hones the technical knowledge of its grant workforce.

DOT operating administrations use methods other than formal courses to train the grant workforce. For example, a FMCSA official said that they have conducted webinars on specific grant issues such as audits and indirect costs. These webinars are recorded and posted to the operating administration's website for others to view. In another example, a FHWA official told us that in addition to formal classroom instruction they encourage other training methods such as on-the-job training, working one-on-one with a team leader, and self-paced learning through instructional resources, such as the *DOT Financial Assistance Guidance Manual*, on agency websites.

Certification

According to agency officials, DOT did not have an agency-wide requirement of a grants management certification for the grant workforce. Also, although some operating administrations offered training that leads to a grants management certificate, none of the operating administrations required certification for their grant workforce.

Other Practices

DOT operating administrations reported that to evaluate their grants training courses offered in fiscal years 2011 and 2012 they

- collected information on participant satisfaction for a majority of the courses offered,
- collected information on knowledge gained in less than half of the courses offered,
- collected information on the impact on individual behavior for seven grants training courses, offered by NHTSA, and
- did not collect information on return on investment for any courses offered.

Appendix II: Overview of Grants Training at the
Departments of Education, Health and Human
Services, State, and Transportation

In order to assess the impact of training on individual behavior, officials at
NHTSA told us that for grants training courses provided by the
Transportation Safety Institute, course participants receive an evaluation
form 90 days after they take the course. This evaluation asks, among
other questions, what the participants have learned from the courses that
has impacted their performance at work and if the courses have better
equipped them to plan, develop, and implement highway safety
programs. The information collected through the evaluations is not
systematically analyzed beyond a basic review although the comments
are considered when updating course curricula, according to NHTSA
officials.

Appendix III: Grant Workforce by Job Series for the Departments of Education, Health and Human Services, State, and Transportation as of June 2013

Series number	Series name	Education	HHS[a]	State	DOT	Total	Percent
1109	Grants Management Series		733	25	1	759	14.81
Foreign Service[b]	Foreign Service			740[c]		740	14.44
685	Public Health Program Specialist		611			611	11.92
343	Management and Program Analysis Series	257	93	6	56	412	8.04
501	Financial Administration and Program Series		200	10	157	367	7.16
1720	Education Program Series	290				290	5.66
2101	Transportation Specialist				187	187	3.65
301	Miscellaneous Administration and Program Series	71	16	7	84	178	3.47
101	Social Science Series	40	115			155	3.02
810	Civil Engineering Series				139	139	2.71
510	Accounting Series		90	10	14	114	2.22
20	Community Planning Series				113	113	2.20
1101	General Business and Industry Series	70	6	21	7	104	2.03
2125	Highway Safety Series				101	101	1.97
340	Program Management Series		8		89	97	1.89
107	Health Insurance Administration Series		86			86	1.68
560	Budget Analysis Series		12	60	8	80	1.56
801	General Engineering Series		2		67	69	1.35
601	General Health Science Series		56			56	1.09
28	Environmental Protection Specialist				50	50	0.98
303	Miscellaneous Clerk and Assistant Series		16		33	49	0.96
2186	Technical Systems Program Manager				44	44	0.86
905	General Attorney Series				41	41	0.80
1730	Education Research Series	33				33	0.64
602	Medical Officer		29			29	0.57
610	Nurse		27			27	0.53
360	Equal Opportunity Compliance Series				27	27	0.53
1102	Contracting Series		8	3	12	23	0.45
341	Administrative Officer				23	23	0.45
318	Secretary		2		15	17	0.33
511	Auditing Series		15			15	0.29
2210	Information Technology Management Series		7		5	12	0.23
344	Management and Program Clerical and Assistance Series				9	9	0.18

Appendix III: Grant Workforce by Job Series
for the Departments of Education, Health and
Human Services, State, and Transportation as
of June 2013

Series number	Series name	Education	HHS[a]	State	DOT	Total	Percent
US Public Health Service Commissioned Corps	US Public Health Service Commissioned Corps		8			8	0.16
808	Architecture Series		7			7	0.14
1160	Financial Analysis Series				6	6	0.12
505	Financial Management Series		1	2	3	6	0.12
2110	Transportation Industry Analysis Series				5	5	0.10
1530	Statistics Series		4			4	0.08
1035	Public Affairs Series		2		2	4	0.08
1701	General Education and Training Series		2			2	0.04
871	Naval Architecture Series				2	2	0.04
830	Mechanical Engineering Series				2	2	0.04
680	Dental Officer		2			2	0.04
401	General Natural Resources Management and Biological Sciences Series		2			2	0.04
185	Social Work Series		2			2	0.04
102	Social Science Aid and Technician		2			2	0.04
950	Paralegal Specialist				2	2	0.04
1170	Realty Series				2	2	0.04
110	Economist				2	2	0.04
1082	Writing and Editing Series				2	2	0.04
986	Legal Assistance Series				1	1	0.02
1801	General Inspection, Investigation, Enforcement, and Compliance Series				1	1	0.02
1529	Mathematical Statistics Series				1	1	0.02
1083	Technical Writing and Editing Series		1			1	0.02
803	Safety Engineering Series		1			1	0.02
346	Logistics Management Specialist			1		1	0.02
	Total	**761**	**2,166**	**885**	**1,313**	**5,125**	**100**

Source: GAO analysis of Education, HHS, State, and DOT data.

Note: The data obtained reflect agency counts taken between December 2012 and June 2013.

[a]For one operating division in HHS, the National Institutes of Health, officials reported the number of grants management professionals that were, or will be, subject to certification. Officials told us that this encompasses the majority of their grant workforce.

[b]Foreign Service officers specialize in five functional areas to meet the needs of individual overseas posts. These include consular, economic, management, political, and public diplomacy.

[c]Does not include grants officer representatives (GOR). State officials told us that they do not yet have a complete accounting of GORs since the program that tracks certified GORs was enacted in January 2013. A full accounting is expected by late summer 2013.

Appendix IV: OPM Grants Management Competency Model

The following competency model was released by OPM in September 2009.[1] According to OPM officials, the model was developed using their standard approach, known as the Multipurpose Occupational Systems Analysis Inventory–Close Ended method. This included several procedures such as announcing the intent to study competencies for the grant workforce, collecting information from agencies, performing environmental scans, speaking with subject-matter experts to refine the competencies and job tasks, and surveying the workforce on which competencies are appropriate for different grades of the grant workforce. In addition, the officials told us that they worked with OMB's Grants Policy Committee to help ensure that the survey employed a common language that the grant workforce across the federal government would understand.[2]

---

[1] This competency model, along with complete definitions of all the terms listed, is available at OPM's website.
See http://www.chcoc.gov/transmittals/TransmittalDetails.aspx?TransmittalID=2515 (accessed March 5, 2013).

[2] Since this is a government-wide model, OPM states that agencies are responsible for conducting job analyses for work responsibilities outside the grants management function. Similarly, agencies must determine the applicability of these competencies to positions which do not perform the full range of grants management work.

Table 6: OPM Grants Management Competencies by Grade Level

General Competencies		
Grade 7	**Grade 9**	**Grade 11**
Accountability	Accountability	Accountability
Arithmetic	Arithmetic	Arithmetic
Attention to Detail	Attention to Detail	Attention to Detail
Computer Skills	Computer Skills	Computer Skills
Customer Service	Customer Service	Creative Thinking
Flexibility	Decision Making	Customer Service
Integrity/Honesty	Flexibility	Decision Making
Interpersonal Skills	Information Management	Flex bility
Learning	Integrity/Honesty	Information Management
Memory	Interpersonal Skills	Integrity/Honesty
Oral Communication	Learning	Interpersonal Skills
Planning and Evaluating	Memory	Learning
Reading	Oral Communication	Mathematical Reasoning
Self-Management	Planning and Evaluating	Memory
Stress Tolerance	Problem Solving	Oral Communication
Teamwork	Reading	Organizational Awareness
Technical Competence	Reasoning	Planning and Evaluating
Writing	Resilience	Problem Solving
	Self-Management	Project Management
	Stress Tolerance	Reading
	Teamwork	Reasoning
	Technical Competence	Resilience
	Writing	Self-Management
		Stress Tolerance
		Teamwork
		Technical Competence
		Writing
Technical Competencies		
Grade 7	**Grade 9**	**Grade 11**
		Compliance
		Financial Assistance Mechanisms
		Grants Management
		Grants Management Laws, Regulations & Guidelines

GAO-13-591 Training the Federal Grant Workforce

General Competencies			
Grade 12	**Grade 13**	**Grade 14**	**Grade 15**
Accountability	Accountability	Accountability	Accountability
Arithmetic	Arithmetic	Arithmetic	Arithmetic
Attention to Detail	Attention to Detail	Attention to Detail	Attention to Detail
Computer Skills	Computer Skills	Computer Skills	Computer Skills
Conflict Management	Conflict Management	Conflict Management	Conflict Management
Creative Thinking	Creative Thinking	Creative Thinking	Creative Thinking
Customer Service	Customer Service	Customer Service	Customer Service
Decision Making	Decision Making	Decision Making	Decision Making
Flexibility	Flexibility	External Awareness	External Awareness
Influencing/Negotiating	Influencing/Negotiating	Flexibility	Flexibility
Information Management	Information Management	Influencing/Negotiating	Influencing/Negotiating
Integrity/Honesty	Integrity/Honesty	Information Management	Information Management
Interpersonal Skills	Interpersonal Skills	Integrity/Honesty	Integrity/Honesty
Leadership	Leadership	Interpersonal Skills	Interpersonal Skills
Learning	Learning	Leadership	Leadership
Memory	Mathematical Reasoning	Learning	Learning
Oral Communication	Memory	Mathematical Reasoning	Mathematical Reasoning
Organizational Awareness	Oral Communication	Memory	Memory
Partnering	Organizational Awareness	Oral Communication	Oral Communication
Planning and Evaluating	Partnering	Organizational Awareness	Organizational Awareness
Problem Solving	Planning and Evaluating	Partnering	Partnering
Project Management	Problem Solving	Planning and Evaluating	Planning and Evaluating
Reading	Project Management	Problem Solving	Problem Solving
Reasoning	Reading	Project Management	Project Management
Resilience	Reasoning	Reading	Reading
Self-Management	Resilience	Reasoning	Reasoning
Stress Tolerance	Self-Management	Resilience	Resilience
Teaching Others	Stress Tolerance	Self-Management	Self-Management
Teamwork	Teaching Others	Strategic Thinking	Strategic Thinking
Technical Competence	Teamwork	Stress Tolerance	Stress Tolerance
Vision	Technical Competence	Teaching Others	Teaching Others
Writing	Vision	Teamwork	Teamwork
	Writing	Technical Competence	Technical Competence
		Vision	Vision
		Writing	Writing

Technical Competencies			
Grade 12	**Grade 13**	**Grade 14**	**Grade 15**
Compliance	Compliance	Compliance	Compliance
Financial Analysis	Financial Analysis	Financial Analysis	Financial Analysis
Financial Assistance Mechanisms	Financial Assistance Mechanisms	Financial Assistance Mechanisms	Financial Assistance Mechanisms
Grants Management	Grants Management	Grants Management	Grants Management
Grants Management Laws, Regulations & Guidelines	Grants Management Laws, Regulations & Guidelines	Grants Management Laws, Regulations & Guidelines	Grants Management Laws, Regulations & Guidelines

Source: OPM.

Appendix V: GAO Contact and Staff Acknowledgements

GAO contact	Stanley J. Czerwinski, Director, (202) 512-6806 or czerwinskis@gao.gov
Staff Acknowledgments	In addition to the contact named above, Peter Del Toro, Assistant Director; Erin Saunders Rath; and Shelby Kain made key contributions to all aspects of the report. Vida Awumey, Thomas Beall, Penny Berrier, Jill Center, Gus J. Crosetto, Beryl H. Davis, R. Eli DeVan, Debra A. Draper, Alexandra Edwards, Robert Gebhart, George Guttman, Melissa King, Belva M. Martin, Kimberly McGatlin, Rebecca Rose, Michelle B. Rosenberg, and Stuart Kauffman also provided assistance. In addition, Amy Bowser provided legal support and Donna Miller developed the report's graphics.

GAO's Mission	The Government Accountability Office, the audit, evaluation, and investigative arm of Congress, exists to support Congress in meeting its constitutional responsibilities and to help improve the performance and accountability of the federal government for the American people. GAO examines the use of public funds; evaluates federal programs and policies; and provides analyses, recommendations, and other assistance to help Congress make informed oversight, policy, and funding decisions. GAO's commitment to good government is reflected in its core values of accountability, integrity, and reliability.
Obtaining Copies of GAO Reports and Testimony	The fastest and easiest way to obtain copies of GAO documents at no cost is through GAO's website (http://www.gao.gov). Each weekday afternoon, GAO posts on its website newly released reports, testimony, and correspondence. To have GAO e-mail you a list of newly posted products, go to http://www.gao.gov and select "E-mail Updates."
Order by Phone	The price of each GAO publication reflects GAO's actual cost of production and distribution and depends on the number of pages in the publication and whether the publication is printed in color or black and white. Pricing and ordering information is posted on GAO's website, http://www.gao.gov/ordering.htm. Place orders by calling (202) 512-6000, toll free (866) 801-7077, or TDD (202) 512-2537. Orders may be paid for using American Express, Discover Card, MasterCard, Visa, check, or money order. Call for additional information.
Connect with GAO	Connect with GAO on Facebook, Flickr, Twitter, and YouTube. Subscribe to our RSS Feeds or E-mail Updates. Listen to our Podcasts. Visit GAO on the web at www.gao.gov.
To Report Fraud, Waste, and Abuse in Federal Programs	Contact: Website: http://www.gao.gov/fraudnet/fraudnet.htm E-mail: fraudnet@gao.gov Automated answering system: (800) 424-5454 or (202) 512-7470
Congressional Relations	Katherine Siggerud, Managing Director, siggerudk@gao.gov, (202) 512-4400, U.S. Government Accountability Office, 441 G Street NW, Room 7125, Washington, DC 20548
Public Affairs	Chuck Young, Managing Director, youngc1@gao.gov, (202) 512-4800 U.S. Government Accountability Office, 441 G Street NW, Room 7149 Washington, DC 20548

www.ingramcontent.com/pod-product-compliance
Lightning Source LLC
Chambersburg PA
CBHW080540290526
45790CB00006B/2483